by Rennie McOwan

PUBLISHING

WRITING *to* REMEMBER

Lang**Syne**

PUBLISHING

WRITING *to* REMEMBER

79 Main Street, Newtongrange,
Midlothian EH22 4NA
Tel: 0131 344 0414   Fax: 0845 075 6085
E-mail: info@lang-syne.co.uk
www.langsyneshop.co.uk

Design by Dorothy Meikle
Printed by Ricoh Print Scotland
© Lang Syne Publishers Ltd 2013

ISBN 978-1-85217-069-1

MacEwan

SEPT NAMES INCLUDE:

Ewan
Ewen
Ewing
McEwen
McKean
McOwan

MacEwan

MOTTO:
Reviresco
("I grow green").

CREST:
The trunk of an oak tree
from which sprout forth
young branches, proper.

GAELIC NAME:
MacEoghainn

Chapter one:

The origins of the clan system

by Rennie McOwan

The original Scottish clans of the Highlands and the great families of the Lowlands and Borders were gatherings of families, relatives, allies and neighbours for mutual protection against rivals or invaders.

Scotland experienced invasion from the Vikings, the Romans and English armies from the south. The Norman invasion of what is now England also had an influence on land-holding in Scotland. Some of these invaders stayed on and in time became 'Scottish'.

The word clan derives from the Gaelic language term 'clann', meaning children, and it was first used many centuries ago as communities were formed around tribal lands in glens and mountain fastnesses.

The format of clans changed over the centuries, but at its best the chief and his family held the land on behalf of all, like trustees, and the ordinary clansmen and women believed they had a blood relationship with the founder of their clan.

There were two way duties and obligations. An inadequate chief could be deposed and replaced by someone of greater ability.

Clan people had an immense pride in race. Their relationship with the chief was like adult children to a father and they had a real dignity.

The concept of clanship is very old and a more feudal notion of authority gradually crept in.

Pictland, for instance, was divided into seven principalities ruled by feudal leaders who were the strongest and most charismatic leaders of their particular groups.

By the sixth century the 'British' kingdoms of Strathclyde, Lothian and Celtic Dalriada (Argyll) had emerged and Scotland, as one nation, began to take shape in the time of King Kenneth MacAlpin.

Some chiefs claimed descent from

ancient kings which may not have been accurate in every case.

By the twelfth and thirteenth centuries the clans and families were more strongly brought under the central control of Scottish monarchs.

Lands were awarded and administered more and more under royal favour, yet the power of the area clan chiefs was still very great.

The long wars to ensure Scotland's independence against the expansionist ideas of English monarchs extended the influence of some clans and reduced the lands of others.

Those who supported Scotland's greatest king, Robert the Bruce, were awarded the territories of the families who had opposed his claim to the Scottish throne.

In the Scottish Borders country – the notorious Debatable Lands – the great families built up a ferocious reputation for providing warlike men accustomed to raiding into England and occasionally fighting one another.

Chiefs had the power to dispense justice and to confiscate lands and clan warfare produced a society where martial virtues – courage, hardiness, tenacity – were greatly admired.

Gradually the relationship between the clans and the Crown became strained as Scottish monarchs became more orientated to life in the Lowlands and, on occasion, towards England.

The Highland clans spoke a different language, Gaelic, whereas the language of Lowland Scotland and the court was Scots and in more modern times, English.

Highlanders dressed differently, had different customs, and their wild mountain land sometimes seemed almost foreign to people living in the Lowlands.

It must be emphasised that Gaelic culture was very rich and story-telling, poetry, piping, the clarsach (harp) and other music all flourished and were greatly respected.

Highland culture was different from other parts of Scotland but it was not inferior or less sophisticated.

Central Government, whether in London or Edinburgh, sometimes saw the Gaelic clans as

"The spirit of the clan means much to thousands of people"

a challenge to their authority and some sent expeditions into the Highlands and west to crush the power of the Lords of the Isles.

Nevertheless, when the eighteenth century Jacobite Risings came along the cause of the Stuarts was mainly supported by Highland clans.

The word Jacobite comes from the Latin for James – Jacobus. The Jacobites wanted to restore the exiled Stuarts to the throne of Britain.

The monarchies of Scotland and England became one in 1603 when King James VI of Scotland (1st of England) gained the English throne after Queen Elizabeth died.

The Union of Parliaments of Scotland and England, the Treaty of Union, took place in 1707.

Some Highland clans, of course, and Lowland families opposed the Jacobites and supported the incoming Hanoverians.

After the Jacobite cause finally went down at Culloden in 1746 a kind of ethnic cleansing took place. The power of the chiefs was curtailed. Tartan and the pipes were banned in law.

Many emigrated, some because they

wanted to, some because they were evicted by force. In addition, many Highlanders left for the cities of the south to seek work.

Many of the clan lands became home to sheep and deer shooting estates.

But the warlike traditions of the clans and the great Lowland and Border families lived on, with their descendants fighting bravely for freedom in two world wars.

Remember the men from whence you came, says the Gaelic proverb, and to that could be added the role of many heroic women.

The spirit of the clan, of having roots, whether Highland or Lowland, means much to thousands of people.

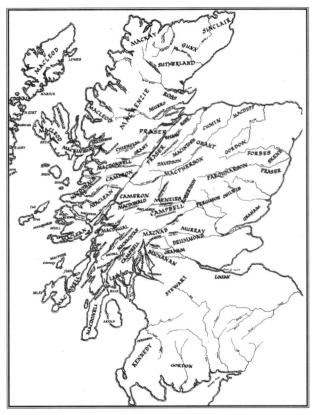

A map of the clans' homelands

Chapter two:

The blood is strong

In the days when the sea and the lochs were the highways, long Loch Fyne in Argyll was of great strategic importance. It gave the powerful Campbells a route to Dumbarton and the Lowlands and the royal seats of power, an influential link denied to the clans of Lochaber and the central Highlands.

Along its shores lived smaller clans, sometimes clinging to their independence, such as the MacLachlans in Strath Lachlan (pronounced Lochlin), who managed to send men to join the Jacobites although surrounded by Hanoverian sympathisers, or the Lamonts who once owned extensive lands and who came under Campbell overlordship and paid dearly when they occasionally joined Clan Campbell's enemies, or the MacNeills who controlled the island of Gigha and parts of Kintyre. Here, too, on Loch Fyne, lived the Clan Ewen.

On the east shore of the loch and to the south of Strath Lachlan, lies a prominent spit of land which sticks out to the west and points towards Asknish on the opposite shore and where that part of the old Campbell territory starts to merge with north Knapdale.

This point of land is marked on the modern maps as Otter Ferry and a ferry did run across Loch Fyne at one time, to Port Ann, south of Loch Gair.

This is the land of the MacEwans, of the Clan Ewen, who centuries ago had territory here. A modern memorial cairn remains the only tangible evidence of their presence.

There are problems in deciding whether a person has an allegiance to Clan Ewen because it does not necessarily follow that every person called Ewen, Ewing, MacEwen, MacOwan, McKean or similar names has an ancient pedigree link with that clan.

It all depends on whether people can trace their family line back to the original Ewens of Otter or to any of the other Ewen communities which later sprang up in different parts of the Highlands and Lowlands and whether they feel sib to the character of Clan Ewen.

Surnames as we know them nowadays were not used in the same way in the past and there is the additional difficulty in ancestry research of 18th and 19th century English or Scots speaking clerks setting down Gaelic names in phonetic English.

People in the past were notoriously careless with spelling and it was not unknown for people to spell their own names in different ways. My own name, McOwan, was once spelled McEwan and although we pronounce it Mac-oan, other call it Makcow-an.

There was always a tradition in the Highlands of people occasionally switching their clan allegiance.

The motto of Clan Ewan is 'Reviresco' which has been translated as 'green growth' in the sense of being ever fresh and alive.

The Lord Lyon, King of Arms, the custodian of Scotland's ancient Lyon Court on heraldic matters, says: "It is perhaps strange that an oak tree was chosen when the name MacEwen derives from the Gaelic MacEoghain, a Gaelic personal name meaning 'born of the yew-tree'. One might have expected a yew stump rather than an oak.

Oak was widely used in boat building and this tree had sacred properties and was burned during festivals such as Beltane, the Celtic new year, and this might have led to the Clan Ewen's choice.

It has also been argued that the name Ewen can mean 'well born' or 'young warrior', and its origin is a matter of complex debate.

To understand the history of Clan Ewen we have to go back to how our nation of Scotland was shaped.

The Romans called the tribal races in what is now Scotland the Picti or painted people because of their tattoo-like war decorations on their body. They also called them the Caledonians, a name which may derive from Celtic words for a wooded stronghold.

These ancient peoples in their small kingdoms have left us a legacy of standing stones, hillfoots, intricately carved inscriptions and designs and jewellery, and traces of a 'language'.

Their native pagan and naturist religions were gradually absorbed by Christianity which was originally brought by missionaries from what is now Ireland.

More and more settlers from Ireland lived on the west coast of Scotland and carved out an enclave for themselves called Dalriada and Dalriata, an area which covered much of modern Argyll. These incomers fought and inter-married with the native Picts in Alba and eventually gave their name, the Scotti, to our nation of Scotland.

The country reached its first, formal unity under King Kenneth MacAlpin in the 9th century.

The MacEwans (Clan Ewen) claim their descent from leaders of the Scotti from Ireland.

It is not easy to chronicle Clan Ewen because they were a broken clan by the middle of the 15th century, there are few records and they have only one – and not prominent – fortified ruin at Otter.

It is known that the ancient Clan Ewen or MacEwen of Otter, in Gaelic Eoghan na h Oitrich, was one of the earliest of the western clans which grew out of the Dalriada Scots.

Chapter three:

Changing fortunes

The MacEwens – says historian and barrister R.S.T. MacEwen – controlled clan territory which at one time measured 25 square miles and at their peak could probably bring over 200 fighting men.

They suffered in the old disputes between Scottish monarchs who desired national control and the powerful Lordship of the Isles and when King Alexander II stamped his central authority on Argyll in 1222 the MacEwens suffered severely through being truculent. The MacNeills got off because they, rightly or wrongly, consented to hold their lands from the Crown.

The MacLachlans also prospered because they had the good sense to marry an heiress of the Lamonts and this increased their power.

But the MacEwens survived. A remnant clung on under their own chief at Otter until their last recorded chief died two and half centuries later.

Not a lot is known about them, but some names are recorded. MacEwen I of Otter, the earliest chief of whom anything is known, lived around 1200. He was succeeded by Severan II of Otter who may have been chief around 1222. The names of the third and fourth chief are lost.

Gillespie V of Otter became chief about 1315 and one wonders if MacEwens fought at Bannockburn in 1314. Another four chiefs are recorded, Ewen VI, John VII, Walter VIII and Sufnee or Sene, the IX and the last of the Otter chiefs.

The "Old Statistical Account of the Parish of Kilfinnan" records in 1750 that on a rocky point on Loch Fyne there stood in 1700 the ruins of Castle MacEwan (Caisteal MhicEoghain), the stronghold of the earlier lords of Otter.

Skene also describes their MacEwen as chief of the clan and 'proprietor' of the northern division of the parish of Otter. A manuscript of 1450, which contains the genealogy of Clann Eoghain na h Oitrich, confirms the clan is derived from Anradan.

By the 15th century things are becoming clearer.

In 1431-32 the ninth chief of Otter, Swene MacEwen (MacCewn), granted a charter of part of the lands of Otter to Duncan, son of Alexander Campbell, a sign that the expansionist Campbells were beginning to exert a pattern of overlordship over their smaller neighbours.

The hand of Scottish kings also played a part in the changing fortunes of Clan Ewen because in 1432 Swene MacCewn resigned the barony of Otter to King James I of Scotland, but received it anew from the King "with remainder" to Celestine Campbell, son and heir of the powerful Duncan Campbell of Lochow (Loch Awe).

Clan Ewen may have opposed King Robert the Bruce in the Scottish Wars of Independence.

The Campbells, who supported the victorious Bruce, grew in their power as a consequence and used their links with the royal line of Scotland to absorb the Clan Ewen lands. By the middle of the 15th century the MacEwens had lost their autonomy, but they had not lost their identity.

Some of the MacEwans joined the Campbells and other western clans. Others made their way to the central Highlands, to Lochaber, and also the islands, including Skye.

Some moved to the fringes of the central Lowlands and settled in Lennox. Others travelled far south and made a new home in Galloway, that southern area which is like the Highlands in miniature. Individual MacEwens crop up all over Scotland.

There was a tradition among the MacEwens of producing bards and poets and sennachies, men of learning and musical skills, who were nurtured in ancient schools of oral learning.

They attached themselves to the Campbell house of Argyll and to the growing Campbell house of Breadalbane and also to the MacDougalls of Dunoillie Castle, near Oban.

The MacEwans who settled in the Lennox country owed allegiance to the Stewart earls and were given grants of land. Between

1625 and 1680 four charters from the dukes of Lennox and Richmond name 'heirs' called 'MacKewin' and 'McEwin'.

Other sources give earlier dates for the Lennox MacEwens and say they fought for Mary Queen of Scots and took part in the battle of Langside in 1568 when the Queen's forces were defeated by the Regent Moray.

They had their own banner which has long since crumbled and vanished.

Local tradition says they had a reputation for strength and a MacEwen clansman was reputed to have carried a stone coffin under one arm and the lid under another from townships at the side of Loch Lomond to the old churchyard at Luss.

Chapter four:

Outlaws and quarrels

There are many families and individuals bearing forms of the clan in Dumbarton, Stirling Clackmannan, Renfrew, Lanark, Ayr and around Glasgow.

A Galloway tale says that about the middle of the 15th century the Agnew Laird of Lochnaw was besieged in the castle on an island in the loch by the men of the Black Douglas. The dispute centred on who should be Sheriff of Galloway.

The castle garrison was about to surrender when their enemies were attacked in the rear by another armed force. The garrison, greatly encouraged, sallied out and the Douglases were chased from the scene. The arrivals were remnants of the McEwans and out of gratitude the laird of Lochnaw gave them the tenantship of four local farms.

When the 1745 Jacobite Rising came along some of the Galloway MacEwens joined

Sir Andrew Agnew on the side of the Hanoverians while others followed Prince Charles Edward Stuart. Tradition has it that when Sir Andrew was besieged inside Blair Castle, in Perthshire, by the Jacobites he was going the rounds when he spoke to one of his soldiers, a man called John McEwen and when they looked out they saw John's brother, Robert, with the Jacobites. Sir Andrew asked John to shoot at Robert, but he refused.

Historian R.S.T. MacEwen also tells of McEwens joining the Royal Navy and also merchantmen, including running cargoes to the West Indies and Africa.

One of them, Robert, became a marine engineer and was the first to erect a steam engine in Russia and was presented by Czar Nicholas with a cup.

McEwens in their different forms, M'Kewan, M'Keown, M'Ewine, M'Ewing, McEwan and McEwen can be identified on graves near Stranraer. Some are believed to have settled on the Isle of Man.

The branch of the McEwens in Lochaber

is known as the Sliochs Eoghain and their ancestry is not clear, but their presence in Lochaber most certainly is. The MacLachlans of Strath Lachlan are also linked to the Camerons.

The name Ewen is very common among the Camerons. In 1219 the name of Sir Ewen de Cambon, third son of the fourth chief, is mentioned in the Chartulary of Arbroath.

The name appears again in the person of Ewen, eldest son of Allan, the ninth chief. This Ewen became tenth chief (1390-96) and took part in the famous inter-clan fight on the North Inch of Perth in 1396.

In 1597 a raid by the Lochaber clans on the Dunbars of Moyness included some MacEwens.

Historians differ about the origins of Clan Cameron, but there was certainly some connection between the Lochaber and Dunbartonshire chiefs and clans. The Privy Council records name Camerons who have the name of 'Ewin' and 'McKewin'.

In 1598 there was a complaint before the Council made by George Dunbar of Clunes (near

Loch Arkaig, in Lochaber) and others against several named MacEwens who were within the area of Cameron control and who are called '200 brokin hieland men and sorneris, all bodin in feir of weir'.

They are described as being armed with bows, daggers, two handed swords, steel bonnets, pistols, muskets and axes. Some of these "broken" McEwens later joined up with the outlawed MacGregors and they lived as brigands. Several McEwans are listed as tenants or supporters of the Mackintoshes and who lived in Lochaber and probably took part in the long running conflict over land ownership between the Camerons and the MacIntoshes.

Another tradition has it that communities of MacEwens settled in Perthshire, around Kenmore (pronounced ken-mur), at the east end of Loch Tay, and they were divided up because of a white horse.

The story goes that the original head of the MacEwans in Perthshire died, leaving two sons who quarrelled over possession of a white horse.

Ownership was decided by whoever could successfully roll a heavy millstone down a hillside by means of a straw rope passed through a hole in the centre.

The successful son got the white horse. The unsuccessful son went off to Ayrshire where he founded another branch of the MacEwens.

My own ancestral line was traced back to the late 1700s and with proven documentation. A likely line, but with less proof and based on the same Christian names being used, ran back to the early 1700s.

Comrie was once famous as a tartan weaving clachan and my ancestors – with the name then spelled as McEwen – were tartan weavers.

They may have been the descendants of Argyllshire MacEwans who moved eastwards with the expansion of the Glen Orchy Campbells into the great house of Breadalbane. One source says some of the Breadalbane McEwens may have attached themselves to the Clan McLaren.

Various spellings of McOwan and

McEwan are common in this glen and appear in 16 of 22 named sites.

The Rev. William A. Gillies, minister of Kenmore from 1912 to 1949, who wrote the much praised book, "In Famed Breadalbane", records little groupings of MacEwans along Loch Tay-side and Loch Earn and the name, or variations of it, still crops up around Crieff and Comrie. The 1769 agricultural survey of Loch Tay-side records 21 MacEwens on land there.

My own theory is that as the Glen Orchy Campbells grew in power and prestige and spread eastwards from Kilchurn Castle at Loch Awe and eventually became Earls and Marquesses of Breadalbane and owned land from Loch Awe to Aberfeldy, that little groups of Ewans of MacEwans also moved eastwards under their influence.

Hill passes link Loch Tay and Loch Earn and also connect Loch Tay-side with glen Lednock and Comrie and records of early weavers in the tartan weaving clachan at Dalginross, Comrie, include people of the name

McEwan. My name, McOwan, was spelled McEwan and my ancestors were listed as tartan weavers.

The name McOwan is also a Hillfoots name and I believe the McOwans/McEwans travelled from Comrie across Strathearn and crossed the Ochils and settled in the Hillfoots villages in Clackmannan, when the weaving mills sprang up at the southern base of the hills in later centuries.

There is evidence, too, of McEwens settling in Skye. It is also known that a handful of MacEwens from Stirling, Perth and Dundee were 'out' and may have been at Culloden. Heraldry attached to the MacEwens can be bewildering and a debt is owed to historian R.S.T. MacEwen who listed the main branches in a history of the clan.

One of the earliest is Ewen or Ewing of Craigtoun who is recorded on a tombstone of 1600 in Bonhill churchyard. These arms belonged originally to Bryson of Craigtoun. Other arms are of later Ewings of Keppoch, Dumbartonshire, and of Glasgow, Levenfield, Louden and Ballikinrain.

The Mucky family claim descent from the MacDougalls of Lorne who were joined by a sept of the MacEwens of Otter.

The McEwans of Glenboig belonged to the Lennox sept. The McEwans of Glasgow belonged to a Renfrewshire family.

There is a McEwan tartan of which the main design is blue/green check similar to the Black Watch and has its origins in Argyll. Red and yellow lines were added in the 19th century. The basic appearance of the MacEwan tartan has links with Campbell influence.

The brewing firm McEwans had a new tartan designed and launched in 1996 to mark the founding of their Fountain Brewery in Edinburgh in 1856 and which is known as "The 1856 McEwan Tartan".

They've long gone now – the days of dozens of MacEwens dressed in a dark tartan and carrying swords and targes and mustering beside their small castle at Otter on Loch Fyne while offshore their war galleys of oak wood swing at anchor.

It is an evocative spot, the site of the cairn beside the shining water of Loch Fyne, and the woods and the hills nearby, and there are still McEwens who gather there and who demonstrate continuity with the great days of the past.

After all, the clan motto means growing again, sprouting greenly with new life and vigour and that is still true.

"Riviresco!"